STATE STUDIES

Uniquely California

Stephen Feinstein

Heinemann Library
Chicago, Illinois

© 2003 Heinemann Library
a division of Reed Elsevier Inc.
Chicago, Illinois

Customer Service 888-454-2279

Visit our website at www.heinemannlibrary.com

Designed by Heinemann Library
Page layout by Depke Design
Printed and bound in the United States by
Lake Book Manufacturing, Inc.

07
10 9 8 7 6 5 4 3

**Library of Congress
Cataloging-in-Publication Data**
Feinstein, Stephen.
    Uniquely California / by Stephen Feinstein.
        p. cm. -- (Heinemann state studies)
    Summary: Examines what makes California
unique, including
  its symbols, flags, songs, recipes, landmarks, and
more.
    Includes bibliographical references and index.
    ISBN 978-1-4034-0344-5 (1-4034-0344-9) (HC)
    ISBN 978-1-4034-0561-6 (1-4034-0561-1) (PBK)
    1. California--Juvenile literature.   [1. Califor-
nia.]   I.
Title.
    II. Series.
    F861.3.F45 2002
    979.4--dc21

2002010882

Acknowledgments
The author and publishers are grateful to the
following for permission to reproduce copyright
material:

Cover photographs by (top, L-R) Mission/
Photophile, F. Folkks/Corbis, Joseph Sohm/
ChromoSohm, Inc./Corbis, Massimo Borchi/Bruce
Coleman Inc., (main) Robert E. Barber/Visuals
Unlimited

Title page (L-R) Gerald & Buff Corsi/Visuals
Unlimited, David Madison/Bruce Coleman Inc.,
Sal Maimone/Photophile; contents page, p. 34B
Bob Ecker/Heinemann Library; p. 4 S. Mission/
Photophile; p. 5T Bill Ross/Corbis; p. 5B Lois
Bernstein/AP Wide World Photo; pp. 6, 7 California
State Archives; p. 9T Inga Spence/Visuals
Unlimited; p. 9B James Blank/Bruce Coleman Inc.;
p. 10T John Muegge/Visuals Unlimited; p. 10B Ken
Lucas/Visuals Unlimited; p. 11T Kjell Sandved;
p. 11B Ed Degginger/Bruce Coleman Inc.; p. 12
John Elk III/ELKJO/Bruce Coleman Inc.; pp. 15, 21,
23 Mark E. Gibson/Visuals Unlimited; pp.16, 25,
27, 29, 30, 33, 45 maps.com/Heinemann Library;
p. 17 Gene Ahrens/Bruce Coleman Inc.; pp. 18T,
22, 32 Gerald & Buff Corsi/Visuals Unlimited;
p. 18B Robert E. Barber/Visuals Unlimited; p. 19
John D. Cunningham/Visuals Unlimited; p. 20
J. Messerschmidt/Bruce Coleman Inc.; p. 24 David
Butow/Corbis SABA; p. 28 Massimo Borchi/Bruce
Coleman Inc.; p. 31 Sal Maimone/Photophile;
p. 34T Robert Holmes/Corbis; pp. 35, 39, 40, 42B
Bettmann/Corbis; p. 36 David Madison/Bruce
Coleman Inc.; p. 37 Michael Brosilow/Heinemann
Library; p. 38 David Bishop/FoodPix; pp. 41, 42T
Disney Enterprises, Inc.; p. 43 Henry Diltz/Corbis;
p. 44 Photophile

Photo research by Amor Montes de Oca

Thanks to expert reader, author, and editor,
Marlene Smith-Baranzini, M.A., for her help in the
preparation of this book. Also, special thanks to
Lucinda Surber for her curriculum guidance.

Every effort has been made to contact copyright
holders of any material reproduced in this book.
Any omissions will be rectified in subsequent
printings if notice is given to the publisher.

Some words are shown in bold, **like this.**
You can find out what they mean by looking
in the glossary.

Contents

The Golden State

What makes California unique? California has many attractions and landforms found nowhere else in the United States or even the world. This makes the state a fun place to visit and enjoyable to learn about.

You can find California's unique attractions all over the state. In the north, redwood trees hundreds of feet tall tower over the land. In addition, the Sierra Nevada are home to Lake Tahoe, which is over 1,600 feet deep. Highway 1 hugs the Pacific coast, jutting around mountains, riding along oceanside cliffs, and going through lush valleys. Mono Lake's **tufa** formations show the salt flats that formed over thousands of years. Yosemite National Park is

This surfer rides the waves of the Pacific Ocean in the California sun.

Hollywood's Walk of Fame is a unique place to visit in California. These sidewalk stars honor not only movie actors but radio, television, and stage performers. They also honor directors, singers, songwriters, and other well-known people in show business.

home to many striking features, including Yosemite Falls, which tumbles down more than 2,400 feet. In no other state will you find **"painted ladies"** lining the city streets or experience the thrill of riding in a **cable car** down a steep hill. Eating California **cuisine** can be a unique experience, too, especially if you eat outside in December!

California is also home to many famous people. Some local favorites include actor Tom Hanks, golfer Eldrick "Tiger" Woods, former U.S. president Ronald Reagan, and astronaut Sally Ride.

Tom Hanks was born in Concord, California, and raised in various cities around the state.

Keep reading to find out more about the attractions, people, and physical features that make this state uniquely California.

California State Symbols

California, like all states, has official state symbols. These are chosen, often by the state government, to represent the unique characteristics of the state.

STATE FLAG

The grizzly bear on California's state flag represents the many bears that once roamed the state. The grizzly bear is also a symbol of strength and independence. The single red star in the upper left corner shows that California, like Texas, was its own country before becoming a state. The white background symbolizes purity. California adopted the current state flag in 1911.

The state flag is based on the Bear Flag flown in 1846 when settlers revolted against Mexican rule of California.

Major R. S. Garnett of the U.S. Army designed California's seal.

STATE MOTTO: *EUREKA*

The state motto comes from the Greek word *huereka*, meaning "I have found it." These words represent the success of the gold miner in California. The California **legislature** adopted *Eureka* as the official state motto in 1963.

STATE SEAL

The official state seal was adopted in 1849. Minerva, the Roman goddess of wisdom, sits in the center. The wheat, grapes, and grizzly bear at her feet symbolize California's agricultural strength and its wildlife. In the background, a miner works along the Sacramento River below the peaks of the Sierra Nevada. The miner symbolizes mining and the **gold rush.** The 31 stars along the top of the seal represent each state—including California—in the United States at the time of California's admittance in 1850. The ships represent trade and **commerce.** The mountains and ocean represent the state's two natural boundaries.

NICKNAME: THE GOLDEN STATE

California's nickname refers to the official state **mineral**—gold. Most of the gold in the state was mined during the gold rush, but California is still a major producer of it. You can find small amounts of this mineral in many parts of the state.

STATE SONG: "I LOVE YOU, CALIFORNIA"

Los Angeles merchant F. B. Silverwood wrote "I Love You, California," and Alfred Frankenstein, a former conductor of the Los Angeles Symphony Orchestra, composed the music. The song was sung in 1914 on the first ship to sail through the Panama Canal on its way to California. In 1951, the state adopted it as its official song.

"I Love You, California"

Words by F. B. Silverwood, music by A. F. Frankenstein

Verse 1

I love you, California, you're the greatest state of all.
I love you in the winter, summer, spring and in the fall.
I love your fertile valleys; your dear mountains I adore.
I love your grand old ocean and I love her rugged shore.

Chorus

Where the snow crowned Golden Sierras
Keep their watch o'er the valleys bloom,
It is there I would be in our land by the sea,
Every breeze bearing rich perfume.
It is here nature gives of her rarest.
It is Home Sweet Home to me,
And I know when I die I shall breathe my last sigh
For my sunny California.

Verse 2

I love your redwood forests—love your fields of yellow grain.
I love your summer breezes and I love your winter rain.
I love you, land of flowers; land of honey, fruit and wine.
I love you, California; you have won this heart of mine.

Verse 3

I love your old gray Missions—love your vineyards stretching far.
I love you, California, with your Golden Gate ajar.
I love your purple sunsets, love your skies of azure blue.
I love you, California; I just can't help loving you.

Verse 4

I love you, Catalina—you are very dear to me.
I love you, Tamalpais, and I love Yosemite.
I love you, Land of Sunshine, half your beauties are untold.
I loved you in my childhood, and I'll love you when I'm old.

Each year on April 6, the state celebrates California Poppy Day. May 13–18 is Poppy Week.

STATE FLOWER: CALIFORNIA POPPY

California adopted the California poppy, or golden poppy, as the official state flower in 1903. Throughout much of the state, the California poppy covers fields and rolling hills in the springtime with a bright golden-orange carpet. It is also known as the flame flower; *la amapola,* Spanish for "the poppy;" and *copa de oro,* Spanish for "cup of gold."

Humboldt Redwoods State Park contains more than 17,000 acres of coast redwoods.

STATE TREE: CALIFORNIA REDWOOD

There are two **species** of redwoods. Coast redwoods are the tallest tree species in the world, some reaching as high as 360 feet. But the giant sequoias in the Sierra Nevada, while not quite as tall as the coast redwoods, are much thicker. The California redwood, when adopted as the official state tree in 1937, referred only to the coast redwoods. In 1953, California revised the law so that the state tree includes both types of redwoods.

California valley quails fly together in groups of up to 60 birds.

STATE BIRD: CALIFORNIA VALLEY QUAIL

The California valley quail is a common sight along the roads and in the countryside of California. As a result, it became the official state bird in 1931. It is a plump gray bird with a plume of black feathers on top of its head.

STATE FISH: GOLDEN TROUT

In 1947, the golden trout became California's official state fish. The golden trout is one of the few **species** that is native to the southern Sierra Nevada. In 1977, the U.S. Congress established the Golden Trout Wilderness Area to protect the fish. In 1978, the federal government added the golden trout to the list of threatened species.

The golden trout now lives in other areas of the United States, thanks to people transporting the fish to ponds and streams near their homes.

STATE INSECT: CALIFORNIA DOG-FACE BUTTERFLY

California became the first state to have a state insect. In 1929, the dog-face butterfly had been chosen as the state insect, but the **legislature** never made it official. Teachers and students at Dailey Elementary School in Fresno helped to introduce the bill that made it official in 1972.

The dog-face butterfly got its name because some people think the pattern on the male's front wings looks like the face of a poodle.

STATE MINERAL: GOLD

In 1965, California also became the first state to adopt a state **mineral.** Gold was the obvious choice because of the important role it has played in the history of California. The **gold rush,** which lasted from 1849 to the mid-1850s, drew thousands of people to California and led to the settlement and development of the state.

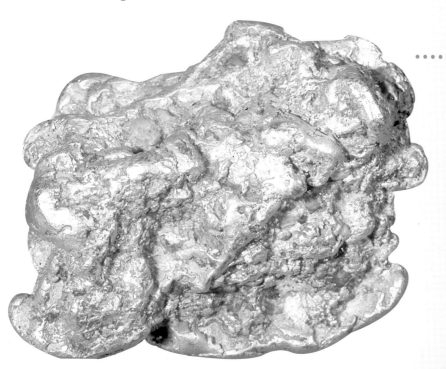

Miners came from all over the world and extracted over 28 million fine ounces of gold during the gold rush. The gold they collected would be worth about $10 billion today.

Government

On September 9, 1850, California became the 31st state to enter the Union. A year earlier, in September 1849, California **delegates** had met in Monterey. They wrote a constitution and declared California a state. That constitution remained in effect until 1879, when the present-day constitution was adopted. More than 350 **amendments,** or changes, have been added to California's constitution since then.

CALIFORNIA'S CONSTITUTION

The California constitution outlines the structure of the state government and protects the rights of its citizens. Some of these rights include freedom of religion, freedom of speech, and freedom of the press. Using New York, Iowa, and other state constitutions as a guide, the delegates wrote a constitution for California with 137 sections. The first copies of it were printed in both English and Spanish. Voters **ratified** the California constitution on November 13, 1849.

California's state capitol building, built in 1874 and located in Sacramento, has undergone many changes over the years.

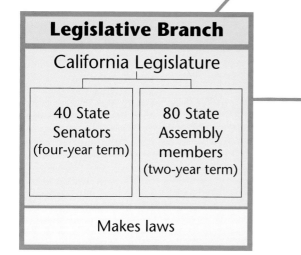

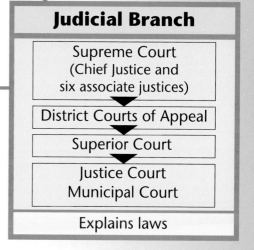

Executive Branch

Governor
(four-year term)

Carries out the laws
of the state

Legislative Branch

California Legislature

| 40 State Senators (four-year term) | 80 State Assembly members (two-year term) |

Makes laws

Judicial Branch

Supreme Court
(Chief Justice and
six associate justices)

District Courts of Appeal

Superior Court

Justice Court
Municipal Court

Explains laws

THREE BRANCHES OF GOVERNMENT

The **executive branch** of California's government carries out the laws. The chief executive is the **governor.** The governor can serve a maximum of eight years. He or she is responsible for seeing that the state laws are carried out. Voters also elect the **lieutenant governor,** the **secretary of state,** the **attorney general,** and the state **treasurer.** All are limited to eight years in office.

The organization of California's state government is similar to that of the U.S. government.

Direct Democracy in California

In California, citizens share the lawmaking power with the state **legislature** in several ways. To propose a new law, citizens use a **petition,** which will be voted upon by the people at the next election. If citizens object to a law passed by the legislature, they can call for a **referendum** by getting signatures of voters on a petition. Voters also can try to remove an elected official from office before his or her term expires by petitioning for a **recall.**

Notable California Political Leaders

Many Californians became major political leaders in the state and then in the national government.

- Earl Warren (1891–1974) was born in Los Angeles. He served as **governor** of California and later as chief justice of the U.S. Supreme Court.

- Dianne Feinstein (1933–), born in San Francisco, served as president of San Francisco's Board of Supervisors and then mayor of San Francisco. In 1992, she became the first woman from California to serve in the U.S. Senate.

- Richard Nixon (1913–1994) was born in Yorba Linda, California. He served as a U.S. representative and as the vice president for Dwight D. Eisenhower from 1953 to 1961. He then became the 37th president of the United States and served from 1969 to 1974.

- Ronald Reagan (1911–), the 40th president of the United States, was born in Illinois. After a distinguished career as a movie actor in Hollywood, he became involved in politics. Reagan was elected governor of California in 1966 and reelected in 1970. He was elected president in 1980 and served for eight years.

The **legislative branch** creates California's state laws. It consists of the state senate and the state assembly. The 40 state senators are elected to 4-year terms and can serve a maximum of 8 years. The 80 assembly members are elected to 2-year terms and can serve up to 6 years.

The **judicial branch** of California's government interprets the state's laws. The California supreme court, the highest court in the state, consists of a chief justice and six associate justices. Each is appointed, or hired, by the governor to a twelve-year term. Voters give final approval to each judicial appointment. Under the supreme court are courts of **appeal,** superior courts, municipal courts, and justice courts.

National Parks

California is home to nine national parks. National parks offer visitors a wide variety of adventures, from historical and **cultural** experiences to natural wonders which can be seen nowhere else on Earth. California is home to the first area set aside for federal protection— Yosemite National Park—and two parks that have the tallest and largest trees in the world.

YOSEMITE NATIONAL PARK

The name *Yosemite* comes from the Native American *uzumati,* or "grizzly bear." Yosemite is located on the western slope of central California's Sierra Nevada range. It has long been recognized as a natural wonder, deserving of

Bridalveil Fall tumbles 620 feet into Yosemite Valley.

California National Parks and Forests

Legend:
- National Park
- National Forest
- National Wildlife Refuge

Oregon

Tule Lake
Lower Klamath
Clear Lake
Modoc
Modoc
Redwood National Park
Arcata
Klamath
Humboldt Bay
Shasta-Trinity
Shasta Lake
Lassen
Six Rivers
Redding
Lassen National Park
Sacramento River
Plumas
Mendocino
Delevan
Colusa
Sacramento
Tahoe
Sutter
Eldorado
Sacramento
Toiyabe
San Pablo Bay
Stanislaus
San Francisco
Yosemite National Park
San Francisco Bay
Inyo
Sierra Nevada
Kesterson
Merced
Sierra
San Luis
Salinas River
Kings Canyon National Park
Monterey
Sequoia National Park
Death Valley National Park
Los Padres
Sequoia
PACIFIC OCEAN
Kern
Bitter Creek
Los Padres
Hopper Mtn.
Angeles
San Bernardino
Joshua Tree National Park
Los Angeles
Cleveland
Cibola
Channel Islands National Park
Salton Sea
Sweetwater Marsh
San Diego
Tijuana Slough
MEXICO

N W E S

0   100 mi.

You can touch the world's largest tree, stand on the lowest point in the Western Hemisphere, and look over North America's highest waterfall in California's national parks.

protection. President Abraham Lincoln set aside the Mariposa grove of giant sequoias in the Yosemite Valley as the nation's first protected area on June 30, 1864. The great naturalist John Muir, who spent years exploring the Sierra Nevada, fell in love with Yosemite. Largely through his efforts, Yosemite became a national park in 1890.

Yosemite's 1,189 square miles are home to many sights. Yosemite Falls is the highest waterfall in North America and the fifth highest in the world. The mountain-face of El Capitan rises 3,593 feet above the valley floor. It is the largest single chunk of **granite** in the world.

BIG AND SMALL TREES

To anyone wandering on the forest floor among the giant redwoods of California, the huge trees seem to reach the sky. Many of the redwoods reach heights of more than 275 feet. The tallest tree in the world is a redwood that stands in Redwood National Park, just south of the Oregon border. It is 368 feet tall—as high as a 30-story building.

Giant sequoias grow in the Sierra Nevada of central California. The General Sherman giant sequoia, the world's largest living tree, grows here in Sequoia National Park. Its trunk alone weighs about 1,385 tons—as much as about 345 elephants.

The General Sherman giant sequoia rises to a height of about 275 feet, and its trunk measures 83 feet around.

Next to the redwoods in the pygmy forests of the northern California coast grow the world's smallest trees—bonsai cypresses and shore pines. Growing in infertile soil, these trees reach their full height at less than eight inches.

The Oldest Trees in the World

Some of California's giant redwoods are more than 3,000 years old. But California's bristlecone pines are even older than that. One bristlecone pine named Methusela is the oldest living tree in the world at around 4,700 years old. You can find these trees in the Ancient Bristlecone Pine Forest, located in the Inyo National Forest on the slopes of the White Mountains. The trees have survived thousands of years of bitter winds in the thin air but have become bent and twisted into odd shapes.

HIGHS AND LOWS

California contains both the highest point in the continental United States and the lowest point in the Western Hemisphere. The highest point is Mount Whitney, located in the Sierra Nevada. It rises 14,495 feet above sea level.

Death Valley is the largest national park in the United States, slightly bigger than the state of Connecticut!

Not more than 80 miles away is the lowest point in the Western Hemisphere—

located in Death Valley National Park. This point is 282 feet below sea level. It is near a place called Badwater, a small pond in a sandy salt flat. It lies between the mountain ranges east of the Sierra Nevada.

In addition to being the lowest point in the Western Hemisphere, Death Valley is also the hottest place on Earth. A record high temperature of 134° F in the shade was recorded on July 10, 1913. In 1974, Death Valley recorded 134 days of temperatures above 100° F. In 1994, there were 31 days over 120° F and 97 days over 110° F.

Point Reyes National Seashore

About 30 miles north of San Francisco is the Point Reyes National Seashore, a 65,000-acre wilderness of forests, mountains, and coastline. This area is unique because of its wildlife. Thirty-seven **species** of native land animals and marine mammals, such as elk, bobcats, seals, and whales, live on the **peninsula** or in the water around it. Over 45 percent of all birds native to the United States are also found here, including rare species such as the California condor.

At certain times of the year, visitors enjoy watching the annual migration of the Pacific gray whale at the Point Reyes Lighthouse.

More Scenic Wonders

There are many more unique sights and natural wonders to see in California. Read on to find out more about one of the deepest lakes in the world, a highway more thrilling than a roller coaster, and one of the largest volcanoes in the United States.

LAKE TAHOE

Along the California-Nevada border, about 6,200 feet above sea level, is Lake Tahoe. It is the largest alpine lake in North America and is one of the deepest lakes in the world. Lake Tahoe holds over 39

Emerald Bay is in the southwest corner of Lake Tahoe. Fannette Island, pictured below, rises 150 feet out of the bay.

trillion gallons of water. If it were to be completely drained, Lake Tahoe could cover a flat area the size of California to a depth of fourteen inches.

Big Sur

Central California's Big Sur country is an approximately 60-mile-long stretch of rugged coastline between San Simeon in the south and Carmel in the north. One of the best ways to see the Big Sur coast is to drive along the Pacific Coast Highway (Highway 1). No other U.S. highway winds around steep sides of mountains that sharply drop off into the ocean below like Highway 1. The Big Sur area is also a safe home for wildlife. **Endangered** California condors and peregrine falcons nest in the area, and thousands of elephant seals come ashore each winter. The nearby redwoods and oak woodlands are also home to many **species** of birds, including the acorn woodpecker.

Highway 1 stretches a total of 644 miles along the California coast. The Big Sur area is shown here.

Henry Miller and Big Sur

The writer Henry Miller (1891–1980) arrived on the Big Sur coast in 1944. He fell in love with the area and lived there for the rest of his life. From his home on a mountainside high above the sea, this is what Miller saw:

> On a clear, bright day, when the blue of the sea rivals the blue of the sky, one sees the hawk, the eagle, the buzzard soaring above the still, hushed canyons. In summer, when the fogs roll in, one can look down upon a sea of clouds floating listlessly above the ocean; they have the appearance, at times, of huge iridescent soap bubbles, over which, now and then, may be seen a double rainbow.

MONO LAKE

In eastern California, just across the Sierra Nevada from Yosemite, lies one of California's most unique physical features—Mono Lake. This huge, gray-blue body of water sits in the middle of vast salt flats in a high desert, more than 6,000 feet above sea level. Just to the south

*Mono Lake's **tufa** formations were formed underwater when salty lake water combined with fresh spring water bubbling up from below. When the lake level dropped, the tufa formations were revealed.*

are twelve volcanoes known as the Mono Craters. Scientists believe that these craters are at the top of the list of U.S. volcanoes most likely to erupt in the near future.

Mono Lake is so salty that early settlers believed nothing could live in its waters. However, California's native **Paiutes** who lived nearby harvested the lake's **brine** fly **grubs,** a good source of protein. Another mystery was the huge population of seagulls and other birds usually found near the sea. The birds were drawn to Mono Lake because it had so many brine flies and brine shrimp for them to eat.

MOUNT SHASTA

Northern California's Mount Shasta, at 14,162 feet, is one of the largest volcanoes in the United States. Covered by snow all year, Mount Shasta towers 10,000 feet above the surrounding countryside. Shasta is an active volcano, but for now it is **dormant.** Mount Shasta last erupted in 1786. Scientists believe it will erupt again sometime in the future.

Over the last 10,000 years, Mount Shasta has erupted about once every 800 years.

Earthquake Country

California rests on shaky ground. The whole state is crisscrossed by earthquake **faults.** Some parts of the state, however, have a greater chance of an earthquake than others. The areas in the greatest danger are also the parts of the state with the most people—the San Francisco area and the Los Angeles area. Parts of these regions lie near or directly on the **notorious** San Andreas Fault.

The San Andreas Fault is the line where two **tectonic plates**—great slabs of the earth's crust—meet and grind together. The Pacific Plate is creeping north by northwest along the North American Plate at about two inches per year. At this rate, in about ten million years, Los Angeles—located on the Pacific Plate—could move next to San Francisco. As the plates grind against each other, the friction causes earthquakes. **Seismographs** are delicate scientific instruments that measure them. Although there are many thousands of earthquakes

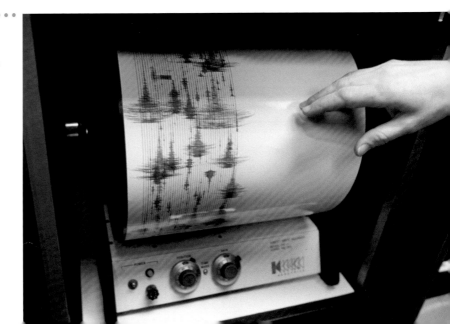

Scientists use seismographs to monitor the strength and patterns of an earthquake's movement.

Earthquake Country

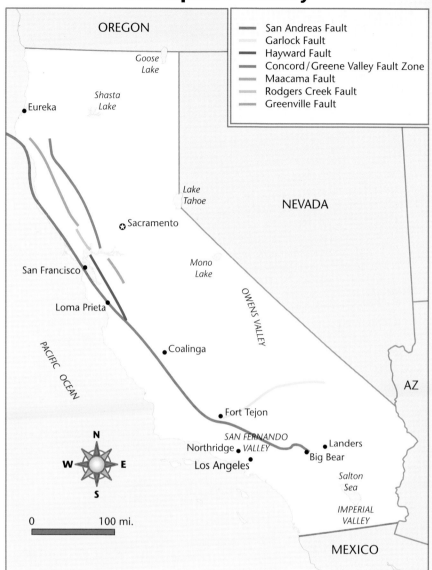

Legend:
- San Andreas Fault
- Garlock Fault
- Hayward Fault
- Concord/Greene Valley Fault Zone
- Maacama Fault
- Rodgers Creek Fault
- Greenville Fault

OREGON
Goose Lake
Shasta Lake
Eureka
Lake Tahoe
NEVADA
Sacramento
Mono Lake
San Francisco
OWENS VALLEY
Loma Prieta
PACIFIC OCEAN
Coalinga
AZ
Fort Tejon
SAN FERNANDO VALLEY
Northridge
Landers
Los Angeles
Big Bear
Salton Sea
IMPERIAL VALLEY
MEXICO

N W E S

0   100 mi.

California experiences more earthquakes than any other state because of the many fault lines running through it.

each year in California, most are too small to be felt. The movement of the plates is slow most of the time. But every now and then, there is sudden, strong slippage along the fault, and serious problems occur.

SAN FRANCISCO, APRIL 18, 1906

The city began to shake just before dawn at 5:12 A.M. on April 18, 1906. Within 60 seconds, it had ended. The earthquake, which measured 8.3 on the **Richter scale,** ruined downtown San Francisco. The earthquake's **epicenter** was located on the San Andreas **Fault,** about 30 miles north of the city.

Major California Earthquakes

Year	Richter Magnitude	Location	Damages	Deaths
1857	8.3	Fort Tejon	unknown	1
1868	7.0	Hayward **Fault**	$350,000	30
1872	7.6	Owens Valley	$250,000	27
1906	8.3	San Francisco	$500 million	3,000
1940	7.1	Imperial Valley	$6 million	9
1952	7.7	Kern County	$50 million	12
1971	6.6	San Fernando Valley	$511 million	58
1980	7.2	Eureka	$1.75 million	0
1983	6.4	Coalinga	$31 million	47
1989	7.1	Loma Prieta (San Francisco area)	$6 billion	63
1992	7.4	Landers/Big Bear	$91.1 million	1
1994	6.7	Northridge (San Fernando Valley)	$10 billion	57

Brick buildings crumbled, and wooden buildings splintered. Broken gas pipes and overturned stoves and gas lamps caused fires all over the city. Entire neighborhoods went up in flames. The earthquake had also broken many of the city's water mains. As a result, firefighters did not have enough water to fight the fires. More than 3,000 people died during the disaster, and it left half of the city's 450,000 residents homeless. Many San Franciscans had to live in tents for a short time, but relief funds soon arrived from around the world.

SAN FRANCISCO, OCTOBER 17, 1989

The San Francisco Bay area was hit again on October 17, 1989, by an earthquake measuring 7.1 on the **Richter scale.** It is known as the Loma Prieta earthquake, because its **epicenter** was at Loma Prieta in the Santa

Cruz Mountains, about 70 miles south of San Francisco. The quake struck at 5:04 P.M. and lasted fifteen seconds. Although not as powerful as the 1906 quake, it caused $3 billion in damage to San Francisco alone. Forty-two of the earthquake's deaths occurred when a section of Interstate 880 in Oakland collapsed on top of motorists stuck on the freeway's lower level. In addition, San Francisco's Marina district went up in flames as many apartment buildings crumbled and gas mains broke.

Major California Earthquakes

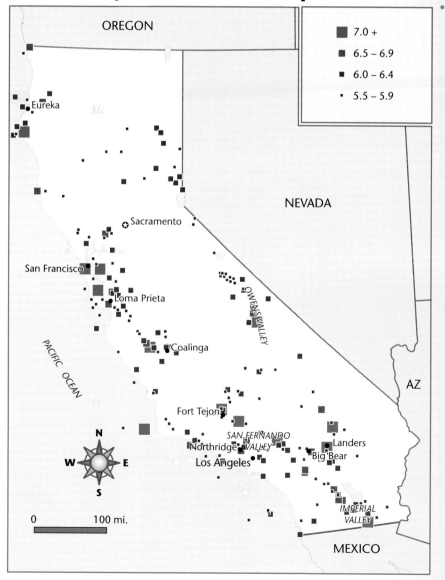

Many of California's earthquakes have occurred along the San Andreas Fault near the cities of San Francisco and Los Angeles. The Richter magnitude is higher along faults.

Unique Cities

Two of California's largest cities—San Francisco and Los Angeles—have unique features found nowhere else.

SAN FRANCISCO

No other city in the United States has as many high, steep hills as San Francisco. From the tops of the city's more than 40 hills, you can see San Francisco Bay, the Pacific Ocean, and many of the area's bridges. Some of the hills rise as high as 376 feet. Riding up and down these steep hills are the city's **cable cars.** The first cable cars were moved by actual cables running overhead. Now, underground cables pull the cars along the track.

In 1873, Andrew Smith Hallidie saw a horse-drawn streetcar slide down a wet, steep hill because of its heavy load. This accident gave him the idea for a safer system for traveling the steep San Francisco hills—cable cars.

San Francisco

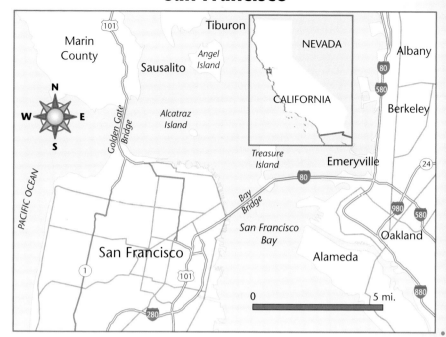

The San Francisco Bay area is the fifth largest metropolitan area in the nation with a population of more than seven million people.

Alcatraz Island sits in the middle of the San Francisco Bay. Alcatraz was home to the U.S. Army's first long-term prison. It became a federal prison in 1934. Its cramped cells housed some of the country's most **notorious** criminals—including Al Capone, the famous 1920s gangster. The federal government closed the prison in 1963 because it was too costly to supply and maintain. Each year, more than one million people tour the site.

Angel Island, also in the San Francisco Bay, was used by the Miwok as a fishing and hunting site for over 6,000 years. Then, from the Civil War (1861–1865) to the 1980s, it housed several military facilities. The government has also used Angel Island as a public health **quarantine** station and an **immigration** station.

Many of San Francisco's residential neighborhoods feature **"painted ladies"**—rows of brightly painted, elegant **Victorian** homes. These homes were some of the first to have indoor plumbing and other items such as porcelain bathroom and kitchen fixtures. Some people believe that the bright colors of the houses reflected the owners' desires to have their houses look as different as possible from the homes they left on the East Coast.

Los Angeles County

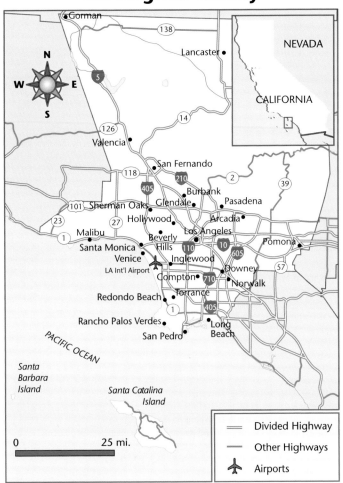

Los Angeles has been called "a hundred suburbs in search of a city" because of its large geographic area and its many neighborhoods.

LOS ANGELES

After World War II ended in 1945, freeways spread out around Los Angeles, and the city grew much larger. Today, Los Angeles County is a seemingly endless sprawl that includes districts such as Hollywood within its 467 square miles. Every part of the city is connected by the freeway system. The huge numbers of cars on the roads create the worst traffic in the country. The average Los Angeles rush-hour driver wastes about 136 hours a year in slow or stopped traffic. The numbers of cars also create thick, polluted air called **smog.** However, when the smog clears, you can see the mountains surrounding the Los Angeles **basin**. On a clear winter day, Los Angeles's palm trees stand against a background of snow-capped mountain peaks and a deep blue sky. The Santa Ana winds that blow in November through January can bring in temperatures as high as 90°F, a unique experience for holiday visitors.

Los Angeles's **cultural** attractions make it a unique city, too. More artists, actors, dancers, musicians, writers, and filmmakers live in Los Angeles than any other city in the world. Los Angeles also has more than 80 stage theaters and 300 museums—more than any other city in the country. The city is also the **mural** capital of the world. More than 1,500 outdoor wall paintings are displayed on buildings, storefronts, and street corners.

Architecture

California is known for its unique architectural styles. Spanish Colonial style can be found throughout the state. This style features white or pastel-colored buildings with red-orange tile roofs, arched doorways, and decorative tiles on the front stairs. Wooden **Victorian**-style homes are also common in California, especially in San Francisco. This style features tall, slender buildings painted in pastel or bright colors, with decorative features in contrasting colors. Elaborately carved details and rounded bay windows are common.

HEARST CASTLE

The Hearst San Simeon State Historical Monument is one of California's most famous destinations. The castle sits on a hill along the central California coast.

*The Victorian-style Carson Mansion in Eureka took more than 100 men two years to build because of its detailed **architecture.***

The Neptune Pool at Hearst Castle is 104 feet long by 58 feet wide and holds 345,000 gallons of water!

William Randolph Hearst, a wealthy newspaper publisher, began building his dream estate in 1919. He and his **architect,** Julia Morgan, worked together on the project for 28 years. They **designed** a Mediterranean hill town using Spanish, **Moorish,** Italian, and French **architecture.**

The *Casa Grande,* or the main house, has 115 rooms, including a movie theater, a **billiards** room, 2 libraries, an indoor swimming pool, and 31 bathrooms. Three other palaces sit on the hilltop, and gardens and fountains surround all the buildings. Hollywood film directors in movies about ancient Rome have used the outdoor pool at Hearst Castle. The castle even has an adjoining zoo!

WINCHESTER MYSTERY HOUSE

Sarah L. Winchester, an **heiress** to the Winchester firearms fortune, became a widow in 1884. Soon after, a **spiritual medium** gave her some bad news—she was

California Attractions

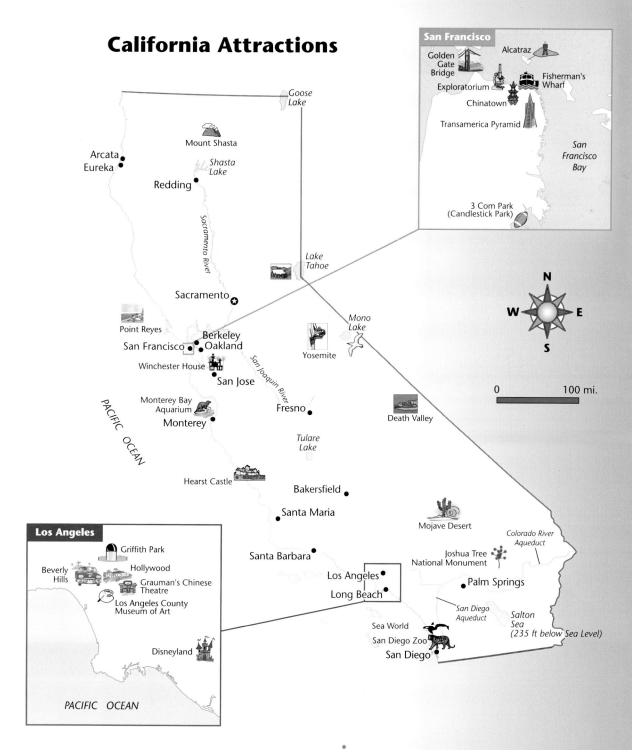

cursed by her **"blood money"** and the spirits of all those shot by Winchester rifles. But the spirits would never harm her as long as she continued construction work on her family home in San Jose. In 1884, the home had eight rooms. For the next 38 years, Winchester added more and more rooms and other details to the home. Hundreds of carpenters

From Mount Shasta to San Diego, you will find plenty of activities in California.

Winchester never had a master set of blueprints, but she did sketch out individual rooms on paper and even tablecloths.

worked around the clock, year after year. By the time work stopped, on the day of her death in 1922, the brightly painted **Victorian** house had 160 rooms. It had 40 stairways, some leading nowhere; 2,000 doors and trapdoors in strange places, with some doors opening into walls; and about 10,000 windows. Some say that Winchester had the house built in this manner to make it so confusing that the spirits would never find her.

THE TRANSAMERICA PYRAMID

The Transamerica Pyramid, completed in 1972, is one of the most **distinctive landmarks** in San Francisco. At first, its strange, pyramid-like shape bothered many San

Franciscans. The building stood out among the more conventional office buildings of the time. However, the architects felt that the building's shape was perfect for skyscrapers. The unique design allowed more air and light onto the streets below it. Over the years, people have grown accustomed to the pyramid's sharp angles. It now seems difficult to imagine what San Francisco would look like without it.

The "wings" on the Transamerica Pyramid house the elevator shafts. After all, elevators need to go straight up.

Bridges

The San Francisco Bay area is home to two of the most impressive bridges in the world—the Golden Gate Bridge and the San Francisco-Oakland Bay Bridge.

THE GOLDEN GATE BRIDGE

The world-famous Golden Gate Bridge—**designed** by **architect** Irwin F. Morrow and his wife Gertrude—connects San Francisco and the Marin Headlands. When the bridge first opened on October 1, 1937, a group of 250,000 people walked across it. At the time, the Golden Gate was the longest and tallest suspension bridge in the world. The bridge is 1.7 miles long. There is a single span of 4,200 feet between the two towers. The 746-foot-

It took 4 years and $35 million to complete construction of the steel and concrete Golden Gate Bridge.

tall towers are equal in height to a 65-story building. The bridge can sway as much as 28 feet during strong winds.

Construction of the bridge was incredibly difficult. The support piers had to be sunk in waters with 60-mile-an-hour **tidal** surges and 15-foot-high swells. Enough concrete was poured into the piers to create a wide sidewalk from coast to coast across the United States. Enough wire to circle the earth at the equator three times was spun into the bridge's suspension cables. Today, about 21,000 cars cross the Golden Gate Bridge each morning. High above the roadway, workers are constantly painting the bridge. When they have finished giving the bridge a new coat of "imperial orange" paint, it is time to begin painting all over again!

THE SAN FRANCISCO-OAKLAND BAY BRIDGE

The San Francisco-Oakland Bay Bridge connects the cities of San Francisco and Oakland. The bridge—one of the longest in the world—is 8.4 miles long, 4.5 miles of it over water. The bridge has two roadways—an upper deck for westbound traffic and a lower deck for eastbound traffic. Its east and west spans are connected by a tunnel through Yerba Buena Island.

The San Francisco-Oakland Bay Bridge was completed in 1936 at a cost of $80 million. At that time, it was the most expensive bridge ever built.

California Cuisine

The food of the most populous U.S. state reflects the **diversity** of California's more than 34 million residents. You can find food from practically every country in the world in California.

California foods have a Mexican influence—ever since the days when the area belonged to Mexico. Tacos, enchiladas, tamales, and burritos are popular dishes in California. They are often served with spicy salsas.

Taste It Yourself

Guacamole, made from avocado, is one of the Mexican-style dishes that are made in California. It has become one of the most popular dips in the country.

Directions:

Slice one or two avocados in half, from stem to bottom. Remove the pit. Scoop the avocado pulp into a bowl and mash it until smooth. Remove peel and seeds from one tomato, dice, and add to bowl. Dice and add green chilies. (Note: More chilies will make a hotter dish.) Squeeze the juice of one lemon over avocado mixture. Add a dash of Tabasco sauce.

Use guacamole for dipping chips or vegetables, or as a spread on burritos or tacos.

Asian **cuisine** is also popular. You can find Chinese, Thai, Korean, Japanese, Indian, Indonesian, and Vietnamese restaurants in most California cities.

CALIFORNIA CUISINE

In the past 30 years, a new style of food preparation has developed in California. Known as California cuisine, it combines parts of many of California's foods. Most important is the use of only the freshest local ingredients—vegetables, fruits, herbs, fish, and dairy products. Hot searing on a grill locks in the flavors of meat, fish, and poultry and keeps the food moist and tender. Combinations of ingredients in a dish—such as black and white sesame seed seared ahi tuna with hot and sour raspberry sauce—are chosen to enhance natural flavors.

Chefs in California also bring together various ingredients because their blending creates a new flavor or texture. Often, parts of a particular cuisine, such as French, are combined with another cuisine, such as Japanese, to create a new dish. These types of combinations—such as grilled Japanese eggplant with spicy garlic goat cheese—are known as fusion foods. Another special type of California cuisine called Cal-Asian food combines American with Asian foods.

Many people enjoy dishes such as this raw tuna salad, an example of a typical California "Cal-Asian meal."

Sports

Among the many unique aspects of California are an array of achievements in sports, including baseball, football, and basketball. California's incredible post–World War II (1939–1945) economic growth also lured two New York baseball teams to the West Coast. The Dodgers moved from Brooklyn to Los Angeles in 1958, and the Giants moved to San Francisco in 1960.

BASEBALL'S GREATEST PITCHER

Sandy Koufax of the Los Angeles Dodgers was one of the greatest pitchers in baseball history. For six years, from 1961 to 1966, he dominated baseball, winning 129 games against 47 losses. Baseball fans shook their heads in amazement at his blazing fastball and swooping curveball. He won the Cy Young award, given to the league's best pitcher, and won 25 or more games three times. Koufax struck out a then major-league record 382 batters in 1965 and tossed no-hitters in four straight seasons. His career World Series earned run average (ERA) of 0.95 also helped the Dodgers to three World Series titles.

Elected to the National Baseball Hall of Fame in 1972, Koufax strikes out fifteen batters in the opening game of the 1963 World Series—a 5-2 Dodger win.

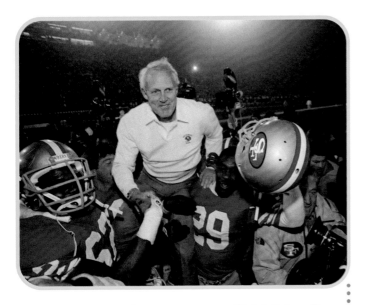

San Francisco players carry Bill Walsh off the field after the 1985 Super Bowl victory.

THE SAN FRANCISCO 49ERS

From 1981 to 1998, the San Francisco 49ers ruled the National Football League (NFL). During that span, they won five Super Bowls and thirteen division titles. Using the timed, short passes of his so-called West Coast offense, Coach Bill Walsh ushered in the era of 49er dominance with a Super Bowl win in 1981.

Joe Montana quarterbacked the 49ers to four of their Super Bowl titles, while Steve Young played quarterback in the fifth in 1994. Both quarterbacks had many talented players around them, including the greatest wide receiver in football history—Jerry Rice. Today, players such as Jeff Garcia and Terrell Owens have maintained 49er tradition with another division title in 2002.

Magic Johnson looks to pass in the first game of the 1980 NBA Finals.

THE LOS ANGELES LAKERS

Another California team—the Los Angeles Lakers—has dominated the National Basketball Association (NBA). During the 1980s, Earvin "Magic" Johnson Jr. led the Lakers to five NBA titles. In game six of the 1980 NBA Finals, Johnson, a point guard, played center. He scored 42 points while leading the Lakers to the championship.

Overall, the Lakers have won the NBA Finals nine times. In 1987 and 1988, the Lakers became the first team in nineteen years to win back-to-back titles. Most recently, led by Kobe Bryant and Shaquille O'Neal, the Lakers have won three straight NBA championships, from 2000 to 2002.

Businesses Born in California

Two **industries** have developed and now dominate the economy of California—entertainment and computers. The film industry started in the early 1900s. After 1910, the industry moved west from New York to Hollywood. Southern California's weather and scenery were better for outdoor filming.

Northern California became the center of the computer industry. The computer revolution began in the 1930s, when Bill Hewlett and Dave Packard started working on electronics in a garage. But the high-tech complex known as Silicon Valley actually began in 1951, with the opening of the Stanford Industrial Park in the Santa Clara valley. The scientists and engineers at Stanford University designed and produced items for Fairchild Semiconductor and Hewlett-Packard.

THE WALT DISNEY COMPANY

Today, the Walt Disney Company is a huge corporation made up of movie studios, the ABC television network,

Over 33 million people visit Disneyland in Anaheim each year.

theme parks, and a cruise line. The original Disneyland Park in Anaheim, California, was built in 1955. Its overwhelming success led to the construction of the Magic Kingdom Park, the Walt Disney World Resort, and the Epcot Center in Orlando, Florida. Disney built other theme parks in Paris and Tokyo. All of this success grew out of the dreams and hard work of a young cartoonist named Walt Disney (1901–1966) and a cartoon mouse named Mickey.

Mickey Mouse

APPLE COMPUTER

In 1976, Steve Jobs and Steve Wozniak had a dream. They wondered whether computers could be made small and cheap enough for anyone to have. At the time, most computers were so big and expensive that only big corporations used them. With their goal in mind, they bought electronic parts and went to work in Jobs's small garage. In six months, they had built the *Apple I*, a revolutionary small computer. By the end of the year, they had sold 150 computers.

Steve Jobs (left), Apple president John Sculley, and Steve Wozniak (right) pose with an Apple IIc *computer.*

Next, they built the *Apple II*, a small computer for personal use. It included a keyboard, a central processing unit (CPU), and a video screen. They introduced the *Apple II* in April 1977. Three years later, sales of Apple computers totaled $139 million. Apple Computer soon became a multi-billion dollar corporation with its innovative line of Macintosh computers.

Hollywood and the Movies

Hollywood is the world-famous center of the movie and television business. Two famous attractions in Hollywood are Universal Studios Hollywood and Grauman's Chinese Theatre.

UNIVERSAL STUDIOS HOLLYWOOD

Universal Studios consists of 413 acres of film studios, theaters, hotels, and office space. More than 500 sets recreate such places as New York City, wild west towns, European cities, Mexican villages, and many other places. Tram rides and river rafts

A mechanical shark from Jaws *leaps toward a tram full of visitors at Universal Studios.*

bring visitors face-to-face with monsters seen in movies. Other thrills include **simulated** explosions, earth-quakes, fires, avalanches, and other special effects.

GRAUMAN'S CHINESE THEATRE

Grauman's Chinese Theatre was built on Hollywood Boulevard in 1927. It was **designed** to look like a Chinese temple. A 30-foot-tall dragon guards the huge entrance. Other dragons are inside the theater. The theater has been the site of more Hollywood movie openings than any other theater. The theater itself has also been used in a number of movies and television shows.

In 1973, Ted Mann bought the theater and named it "Mann's Chinese Theatre." In 2000, Warner Brothers bought it and restored its original name.

People visit the theater just to see the courtyard. Pressed into the concrete floor are the foot-prints, handprints, autographs, and even **mementos** of many famous Hollywood stars.

Nearby, at the corner of Holly-wood and Vine, is the Walk of Fame. More than 1,800 names of Hollywood celebrities are engraved there in bronze stars set into the sidewalk. Some famous Californians featured include Ronald Reagan, Tom Hanks, Walt Disney, and Shirley Temple Black. Gene Autry has the most stars, with his five. Even Big Bird and Lassie have stars.

Map of California

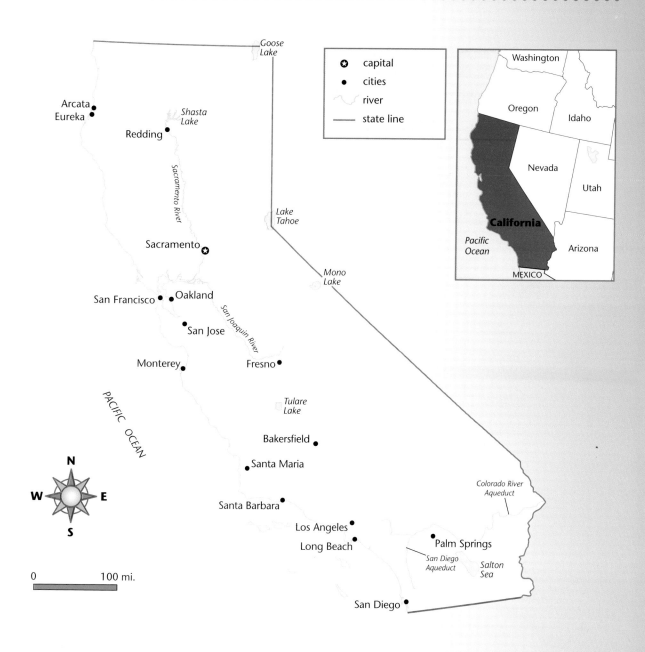

Legend:
- ✪ capital
- • cities
- river
- — state line

Goose Lake

Arcata
Eureka

Shasta Lake

Redding

Sacramento River

Lake Tahoe

Sacramento ✪

Mono Lake

San Francisco • Oakland

San Joaquin River

San Jose

Monterey

Fresno

PACIFIC OCEAN

Tulare Lake

Bakersfield

Santa Maria

N
W E
S

Santa Barbara

Los Angeles

Long Beach

Colorado River Aqueduct

Palm Springs

San Diego Aqueduct

Salton Sea

0   100 mi.

San Diego

Inset map:
- Washington
- Oregon
- Idaho
- Nevada
- Utah
- **California**
- Pacific Ocean
- Arizona
- MEXICO

Glossary

amendment change in, or addition to, a bill or law, such as an amendment to a constitution

architecture designing and building structures. A person who designs buildings is an architect.

appeal ask for a review of a case by a higher court

attorney general chief law officer of a nation or state

basin land drained by a river and its branches

billiards game in which balls are struck by a cue into pockets at the edge of a flat table

blood money money gotten at the cost of another's life

brine saltwater

cable car vehicle on tracks, moved by a cable

commerce buy and sell goods

cuisine style of cooking

cultural ideas, skills, arts, and a way of life of a certain people at a certain time

delegate person sent to a meeting to represent a community

distinctive noticeable

diversity having variety

dormant temporarily inactive

endangered threatened with extinction

epicenter part of the earth's surface directly above the focus of an earthquake

executive branch branch of government that makes sure laws are carried out

fault crack in the earth where movement takes place

gold rush influx into California of many thousands of miners after gold was discovered at Sutter's Mill in January 1848

governor head of the executive branch of a state government.

granite hard rock made largely of crystals of quartz

grub insect larva

heiress woman who inherits somebody's property

immigration act of moving to another country to settle

industry group of businesses that offer a similar product or service

judicial branch branch of government that includes the courts. The judicial branch explains or interprets the laws of the state or nation.

landmark important place or building that people recognize

legislative branch branch of government that makes the laws

legislature governmental body that makes and changes laws

lieutenant governor second-in-command of a state, after the governor

memento something that serves as a reminder

mineral solid substance formed in the earth by nature and obtained by mining

Moorish relating to the Arab conquerors of Spain

mural picture painted on a wall

notorious having an unfavorable reputation

painted lady brightly colored Victorian house

Paiutes Native American tribe

peninsula piece of land extending over a body of water

petition formal written request made to an official person or government body

quarantine holding people in a certain area to prevent the spread of disease

ratified given legal approval

recall act of removing a government official from his or her position by the vote of the people

referendum letting voters approve or disapprove laws

Richter scale scale for measuring an earthquake

secretary of state public official responsible for keeping state records

seismograph instrument that measures vibrations within the earth

simulated made to look like

smog foggy air that is made heavier and darker by smoke and fumes

species group of living things that resemble one another, have common ancestors, and can breed together

spiritual medium person believed to be a channel of communication with the world of spirits

tectonic plates interlocking pieces of land that make up the continents on Earth

tidal ebbing and flowing with the tides

treasurer person in charge of the money of a government

tufa rock formed at the deposit of a river or stream

Victorian a style characteristic of the reign of Queen Victoria (1837–1901) of England

More Books to Read

Burgan, Michael. *California.* Estes Park, Colo.: Benchmark Investigative Group, 2002.

Heinrichs, Ann. *California.* Danbury, Conn.: Children's Press, 1998.

Ingram, Scott. *California: The Golden State.* Milwaukee: Gareth Stevens, 2002.

Welsbacher, Anne. *California.* Edina, Minn.: ABDO Publishing Company, 1998.

Index

About the Author

Stephen Feinstein is a writer of educational materials, specializing in social studies and language arts. His extensive experience in observing and writing about historical, geographical, political, and cultural trends has given him special insights into creating concise yet informative presentations of complex subjects. He lives in Marin County, north of San Francisco, California.